__The Guide to Career Preparation__ is dedicated to my family (Keevia, Kevin, Kelsey and Kev1), who allowed me the freedom and flexibility to expand my life's work. I love you ALL!

The Guide to Career Preparation

This practical guide is written to assist young adults and entry level professionals in securing their first income producing position or taking the next step within chosen career paths. Additionally, tips on fiscal responsibility and learning acuity along with a multitude of other subjects are mentioned to enhance life skills and the knowledge base of individuals and seminar participants. The Guide to Career Preparation should be reviewed as an educational supplement for those starting their careers. For seminar and lecture series associated with this guide contact Creative Concepts in Education, Rockwall, TX.

The Guide to Career Preparation

Employment Search and Success

Sundra Stubbs

outskirtspress

DENVER, COLORADO

Outskirts Press, Inc.
http://www.outskirtspress.com

ISBN: 978-1-4327-9297-8

Outskirts Press and the "OP" logo are trademarks belonging to Outskirts Press, Inc.

PRINTED IN THE UNITED STATES OF AMERICA

Table of Contents

Employment Search

Career Preparation should begin with a thorough evaluation of one's skills and abilities. For young adults, this can be achieved with personality assessments to determine strengths if a knowledge of relevant work place skills is not known or hasn't been validated by proven success in employment or life experiences. Once assessment is complete, various career fields are recommended based on results. From these choices one or two should be narrowed by individual and pursued.

After a general field has been selected to pursue, a position within the field can be obtained usually based on skill set, experience, education or a combination. Proper training and education within the field is highly recommended. Therefore, factor the time needed to complete required education or training. This guide also contains informative tips on education options and funding sources.

After training, education or experience, the desired position can be applied for usually through company's application process (online application, paper application, resume submission etc.). The application, resume, references and interview techniques should be readied in anticipation of a job interview. These items are of the utmost importance for landing a career.

THE APPLICATION—Make certain each item on the application is complete and accurate.

THE RESUME—Derive this information from work history, volunteerism, skills or education.

The REFERENCES (3)—Seek the permission of instructors, employers, community leaders to utilize them as references.

The INTERVIEW—Prepare yourself by mock interviewing with a family member or instructor.

The THANK YOU—Write a letter of thanks to the interviewer to follow up the interview.

Once you have prepared all these items and if you are a good fit for the position(s) you should begin to receive offers of employment. This is the first step in your career! Within your career you may have more than one position as we no longer live in an age of lifetime employment with one employer. In this guide, transitioning employers and job loss are discussed.

A list of possible interview questions is being provided for additional practice.

1. Tell me about yourself.
2. Why did you choose this company to make application?
3. What is your favorite job within this industry and why?
4. How has your education prepared you for this position?
5. How would your instructors describe you? What would they say?
6. What are your strengths?
7. What are your weaknesses?
8. Do you work best alone or as part of a team?
9. What qualities do you feel a successful manager should possess?
10. What is important to you in a job?
11. If I were to hire you, what would you do to make sure you are a fit for our team?
12. Tell me how you might deal with an upset customer.
13. If someone is absent and you must cover multiple positions, what is your plan?
14. Tell me about a situation in which you were under pressure and how you handled?
15. Describe a conflict you had with an employer or instructor.
16. What do you know about this company?
17. How do you deal with situations which may make you late or absent for work?
18. Are you currently employed?

19. If you are employed, why are you leaving your job? If no, why did you leave?

20. What motivates you?

21. How do you define success?

22. What goals have you set for yourself in the future? How do you plan to achieve them?

23. Are you entertaining other job offers at this time?

24. What are your salary requirements?

25. Why should I hire you?

Have three (3) questions prepared for interviewer:

1.

2.

3.

(Tip: Research the company in advance and base your questions on the data found.)

(Tip #2: Discuss salary only if mentioned by employer of after employment offer is made.)

What do I have to offer an employer?

To prepare for resume writing and the interview, derive a list of ten (10) of your strongest attributes, skills and characteristics. Have this listing available when writing your resume for quick reference and for familiarity during the interview process. This will be a valuable resource and a time saver.

1.

2.

3.

4.

5.

6.

7.

8.

9.

10.

Customer Service with Professionalism

It is my belief that no individual should be without basic customer service skills training, regardless of position or industry. The information shared in this guide on customer service is sufficient for ground floor position through entry level positions. The causes/effects of the "over & beyond" principle are explored. Exercises to confirm customer service importance regardless of the job/career or industry are also reviewed.

Customer Service is a skilled approach of handling a customer. Merits of excellent customer service will be gained by both customer and business. The interaction may or may not include a paid transaction.

- Importance of Customer Service
- My role and Customer Service

Customer Service Benefits/Effects:

- Customer Loyalty/Return Business and profitability
- Good service produces happy customers

Over and Beyond Principle:

- Going "over and beyond" or doing more than what is expected at work is best.
- Doing more than what is expected indicates your willingness to work/excel.
- Doing more than expected shows your desire to assist customers.

Customer Service and Me (Exercise)

Base the answers to these questions on your current or most recent job experience or volunteerism.

What is your current job title?

_____

How is customer service a part of your job?

_____

How might making improvements to customer service benefit customers?

_____

How might making improvements to customer service benefit your company?

_____

What changes can you make to incorporate the improvement?

_____

Make the change(s) TODAY!

Networking

This information will assist individuals in identifying potential assistance within their communities, organizations, schools, workplaces, social settings that could potentially enrich their lives with available opportunities. Individuals learn the importance of speaking with various individuals and organizations on their own behalf and on the behalf of others (organizational purposes).

Networking is interacting with others in a social (or sometimes electronic) setting for the purposes of making your identity, skills, abilities and willingness known to others for purposes of employment, gathering support, garnering assistance with organizations or causes.

WHY IS NETWORKING IMPORTANT?

Networking is growing increasingly more popular due to the socialistic nature of our society.

WHY SHOULD I NETWORK?

- Gain confidence
- Establish support/relationships
- Foster assistance for available opportunities

Is networking worthwhile?

- Some employment opportunities (past/present) are found networking.

Formal/Informal networking

- Word of mouth, casual conversation can be termed as "Informal" Networking.

- Meetings, Gatherings, Electronic Social Networks are known as "Formal" Networking.

Online Networking/Cyber Networking

- Using blogs, websites for job seekers, social networking sites/online contacts:

- Gather/share information regarding positions/hiring companies

- Place general information (resume/profile) for possible employment matches

- Common social sites that highlight employment or interest posts

- Serious dedication and clarity required with cyber networking

- Brevity with resume content of sensitive information (recommended for security/safety)

NETWORKING EXERCISES

EXERCISE #1

Interview a partner utilizing frequently asked interview questions from Employment Search section of this guide. Listen intently. You will be responsible for introducing your partner and answering the questions about him/her.

EXERCISE #2

Mock Social Networking Scene: Please use name tags and have prepared three (3) positive attributes about yourself / your employment or your goals that you would like to communicate with others.

EXERCISE #3

Create a professional page about yourself on a social networking website. The purpose of this page is to land an interview for a job within your chosen field/company. The initial draft will be written, prepare to share with group. The final can be published if you so desire!

Market You

Marketing analysis, assessments and behavior models (self assessments determining what each personality type enjoys) and individually created/developed personalized networking channels will assist individuals in formulating their own marketing plan. The individual marketing plan can be used for marketing to perspective employers, social organizations, clubs, etc.

SELF-ASSESSMENT:

What do I enjoy doing in my leisure time?

What subject do/did I most enjoy in high school or college (if no relevant work experience available)?

What task would I be willing to perform with or without pay?

Do I have any practical experience performing this task for others?

_____

Have I only performed this task as a hobby?

_____

Development of Personalized Networking Channels:
Use the networking selections from the Job Search section and create
a list of your channels.

I will use the following contacts to develop networking channels for
myself:

_____

_____

_____

_____

_____

_____

_____

_____

_____

When engaging these contacts using the referenced channels, it is important to remember that marketing yourself can be for purposes of employment (present or future), social affiliation (clubs, organizations, charitable/community events present or future) or Spokesman roles (representing others as well as yourself in some capacity). Therefore, present yourself as polished and professional as possible. You never know what opportunity may arise from this interaction.

What additional contacts can you derive (perhaps from family, friends or other affiliations)?

_____

_____

_____

_____

_____

Career Motivation

Career motivation focuses on developing natural talents, perfecting acquired skills and furthering career altitude via upwardly mobile aspirations and "honing" an individual's best characteristics. It is through an exploration of specific character traits and attitudes, concentration on "initiative" and determination within their chosen career field that reinforces personal motivation.

WHAT ARE "NATURAL TALENTS"?

- Skills/Abilities within individual that were not "learned"
- Qualities that an individual possesses without necessary study
- Effortless characteristics that are part of personality

"ACQUIRED SKILLS" DEFINED:

- "Learned" abilities
- Skills which required study/practice

What comprises Career Altitude?
The components that determine career level are *ability* and *attitude*.

ABILITY

- Determine your natural talents – maximize usage of these talents
- Remain attentive and perfect the acquired skills – utilize these relative to profession
- Seek others for feedback on your personality characteristics –use info to your benefit

ATTITUDE

- "Honing" of additional character and personality traits
- Willingness/desire to learn, grow/stretch yourself
- Learning and redefining "Initiative" as it relates to you

What Is Initiative?

Having the ability to determine what needs to be done, courage to perform the task-AND stepping UP to do so!

STEPS:

1. Identify the problem/concern and who is affected.
2. Devise a plan, course of action for you and others to effectively address.
3. ACT upon your plan while influencing others to assist.

Goals/Attainment

Individuals review a full circle analysis of themselves and their vision for future (personal and professional lives interconnected). A current assessment and projection is done.

Conclusions are then drawn on what would be required to reach the desired goals.

Current Assessment Chart

Projected Goal Assessment (5, 10 year)

Assessment is an analysis of one's own goals, interests, skills, and experience.

Types of Goal Assessments:

- Current Assessment is a review of present day education, experience and achievements.
- Projected Goal Assessment is an estimation of education, experience and goals for future.

An assessment should be evaluated against a current baseline.

The projected 5 or 10 year goal assessment (what individual would like to have achieved).

If no obstacles existed (money, education/training, physical limitations, geographical boundaries) –

- WHAT WOULD BE YOUR GOAL(s) (PERSONAL AND PROFESSIONAL)?

- HOW WOULD YOU GO ABOUT ACHIEVING THIS GOAL (PLAN/STEPS FOR ACTION)?

- WHO WOULD YOU WANT TO WITNESS YOU REACHING YOUR GOALS?

- HOW LONG WOULD YOU BE WILLING TO DEVOTE TO OBTAINING THIS GOAL (s)?

- WHAT CAN BE DONE BY YOU TODAY TO TAKE THE FIRST STEP TOWARDS THAT GOAL(s)?

Goals/Attainment Assessment (Current)

What is your educational level?

What is your employment experience?

What is your interest/passion in life?

What is your dream job?

Goals/Attainment Assessment (5 year Goal, 10 year and beyond)

What is your educational level?

What is your desired education level?

What is your employment experience?

What employment opportunity do you envision for yourself in 5 years?

What employment opportunity do you envision for yourself in 10 years?

What is your interest/passion in life?

What is your dream job?

Tips for Goal Achievement

Clarify Your Objectives:
We are more likely to achieve good to excellent results with a plan rather than without a plan.

Well defined objectives in life provide focus and direction and aids in achieving goals.

- **Establish goals early**
- **Make plans to reach your goals**
- **Monitor progress periodically**
- **Realign when necessary**
- **Persist in your endeavors**
- **Don't QUIT!**

Character and Personal Development

Modeling positive character traits in life as well as within your career will inspire others around you to do the same and compliments your workplace image. Some examples are citizenship, respect, trustworthiness and compassion. Although these may seem to be very basic traits acquired early in the lives of most individuals it is worth mentioning within the context of careers. An individual who respects the opinions and differences of others, along with demonstrations of consideration and tolerance prove more positive than an individual unable to be flexible.

Job Loss / Change

Job Loss/Change information demonstrates to Young Adults ways to effectively recognize change paradigms and shifts within an organization and adjust accordingly. Job loss should be seen as a stepping stone within the individual's career and promote desire to move forward if job loss should occur due to downsizing/layoffs, etc. It is also beneficial to note that change of job should not affect an individual's comprehensive career or credentials and should therefore not be feared. Alternatively, a well written resume should address any employment absences and can also be elaborated on in an interview if employer has concerns.

Effective Communications

Basic communication skills are needed in school, organizations, workplace and life. However, the value of concise, open and polished communication (both written and spoken) should be viewed as one of the most important factors in career success and possibly in life. An individual's ability to properly articulate their viewpoints, ideas, and needs can determine a great deal within their career. To achieve this, it would be beneficial to have a good understanding and command of the English language and vocabulary.

Oftentimes, it is the impeccable ability to effectively communicate that opens doors and catapults careers. Narratives and speeches (both impromptu and prior print) allow individuals to "model" public speaking. It is important for individuals to take opportunities to make a public address to defray "stage fright". This public address could begin as simply as a high school student council endorsement, an oral presentation of a college paper, or role as an announcer within social or organizational groups and should continue throughout life.

If any one opportunity could be afforded to all, it should be practical and continued training in English and effective communication for career advancement and as an imperative life skill.

Attitude and Attire for Workplace

Dialogue and scenarios are explored through role play to demonstrate preferred methods of communication and actions in the workplace. Proper dress/attire in the workplace is covered to ensure individuals recognize the importance of "dressing for success".

Attitude is an outward display of actions, feelings or moods. This can in turn determine the actions, feelings or moods of others. Attitude is the way we convey mood.

TIPS for Attitude Improvement:
- ✓ Employ "faith based" actions (practice positive self-talk).
- ✓ Surround yourself with "positive" people, not negative doubters.
- ✓ Visualize success and chances are good that you will achieve success.
- ✓ Your attitude can either build you up or tear you down...it's your decision.
- ✓ Positive attitudes at work establish a sense of team spirit and increase productivity.

✓ Positive attitude equals positive results; Negative attitude equals negative results.

✓ Attitude can determine your ALTITUDE: don't be restricted by yours!

✓ Attitudes can be contagious...

Attire for the Workplace: Dress appropriately at all times. Your outward appearance is sometimes the only impression others have of you if they don't work directly with you. It is definitely important to dress for the next level of success, not always your current position.

Workplace Attitudes...What Would You Do?

Contemplate these scenarios and determine what your reaction **should** be...

> ➤ Meetings in which most of the discussion is on what is going wrong rather than ideas on how to resolve the problem.

> ➤ Break room complaints about how company is being run and how company is "taking advantage" of employees.

> ➤ General conversations around the workplace in which employees complain to each other that they "hate their jobs".

> ➤ Employees backstab each other in attempts to "get ahead" within the company.

> ➤ Customers receive poor service due to the negativity of the company representatives.

> ➤ Upper management allegedly cares only about how they are measured (short term profits rather than long term company success).

Acuity

Sharpness and clarity of thinking, memorization and study are evaluated, further developed and sometimes challenged via assessment, skills correlation or instruction/written content in employment. These methods can be used to improve any level of academic readiness in career education by utilizing:

- Study Techniques/Improvements

- Memory Enhancement Techniques

- Learning and Attention Additives

- Intelligence Nurturing (High School/College Preparatory learning)

- Emotional IQ Exploration

- Awareness of Learning Barriers: Conflict/Anger Management, Stress Reduction

Stress Management and Life Skills

Within an individual's career various methods to manage stress including development of healthy coping strategies should be utilized. Exploration of breathing and relaxation techniques (mind and body) to relieve tension is recommended to determine what works for each individual. Stress relief on the job can be achieved via brief walks during break, writing, talking techniques, hobbies, meditation and drama/comedy. Relaxation aids and tools (stress balls and gazing cubes) are suggested for integration into work/school day forging laughter and rejuvenation.

Peer-2-Peer Counsel/ Advocacy

Another aspect of career development should be positive work or school relationships. The individual's engagement of their peers through guided, factual instruction or positive reinforcement (when needed) helps with all issues. From matters regarding career development, peer pressure and other subjects it is usually helpful to seek an advocate. The Peer-2-Peer Counsel/Advocacy is a good method of soliciting support. This dynamic experience is especially suitable for different personality types to gain opinion of a trusted peer who may have firsthand knowledge of work environment/culture and players involved. The setting should encourage strictly voluntary participation and encourage opportunities for each person to be both advocate and recipient of counsel at alternate intervals.

Drop-Out Prevention/ College Preparatory

This section of the career guide is for young adults and returning students to provide insight into the importance of remaining not only 'in school' but DEDICATED to academic excellence. Information assists in resisting negative influences that may advocate early departure from school. College preparatory information on federal aid (grants, work study, scholarships and student loans) is reviewed for those interested in higher education.

Importance of Education/Academic Excellence:

- Education is the key to success. (This quote is widely used, but remains true today.)
- Skills and Information acquired in education advance you in life. (Personal and professional life)
- Education cannot be stripped/removed, lost or misappropriated.
- Economic and (sometimes) social playing fields are leveled with the influence of Education.

The achievement of educational goals and resilience to early "outs" from school (high school or college) creates: success, equal footing, and an ability to produce positive outcomes, contributions and talent.

Academic Excellence is the pursuit of highest educational attainment level and the best ranking/quality within those levels achieved. This should be the goal each individual to reach their own "personal best".

DROPPING OUT... **WHAT'S GOOD ABOUT THAT???????!!!!!!!!!!!**

The hype surrounding early departure from school is simply "hype". Let's review the options.

Leaving school early (without benefit of a high school or college degree) versus completion:

- No credentials mean less earning potential (now and future).
- More idle time spent on "non-constructive" tasks versus expanding your knowledge.
- Increased amount of time to "hang with friends" rather than advancing your talents.
- Idle, extra time becomes rapidly boring (especially as you age) unless you have "purpose".
- Decreased or lacking "purpose" in life quickly drains humans and brings on depression.

Keys to avoid the Drop Out "hype":

- Remain/Excel in school.
- Go to college/trade school and find your life's "purpose"!

COLLEGE BOUND... ROAD TO Higher Learning!

Money for College

If training or education is a factor affecting an individual's ability to land a position within their chosen career field, the information provided in this portion of the guide is devoted to resource identification.

College Expenses Worksheet (interactive worksheet to "forecast" expenses)

- Imagine yourself away at college, write down all your "everyday" expenses for a week
- Saving for college
- Personal savings fund accumulated since high school
- Family saving fund or contribution (if applicable)
- High School Graduation Gifts/Funds

Government Federal Student Aid programs (info and forms can be ordered at 1-800-433-3243) or online at www.fafsa.gov or www.Studentaid.ed.gov.

- Work Study
- Pell Grants
- State Grants

Tapping into various other funding sources:

- Scholarships (community/organization sponsored)
- Grants (additional free/provisional funds)
- Fellowships/apprenticeships (offered by departments/ specialty disciplines)

Student Loans

- Government student loans for educational assistance
- Subsidized and Unsubsidized student loans (low interest rates)

Fiscal Responsibility: Money Management

Banking Basics and Savings:

Choose a Bank (Use computer searches, telephone, existing relationships held) to determine

- student checking (if applicable), saving or other suitable account
- seek financial institutions with little/no fee structure
- seek financial institutions with little/no minimum balance requirement
- determine number of ATM/Debit transaction limits and attempt to forecast your usage

Choose an account type (economical or free and specific to your needs)

- Will you use the account to save or as a utility account (taking money in/out)?
- If utility account, will you write checks at all or will you only use ATM/Debit?
- If utility account, sit down and determine how many times/monthly you may withdraw.

How to properly use a Checking account/ATM or Debit cards (balancing)

- Budget only the amount of money that is contained in your account.

- Never attempt a withdrawal/transaction for an amount that is not in your account.

- Attempting to access an amount in excess of the funds in your account is overdraft.

- Debits/Credits: Add and subtract the amount you deposit / withdraw to "balance".

Choosing between banks and credit unions

- Banks are good for building relationships, a wider variety of services and fees to accompany.

- Credit Unions are usually more flexible, may offer fewer services but lower fee structures.

Saving strategies/tips

Always provide yourself an amount of money that you consider "savings".

Designate a percentage or particular dollar amount for savings each pay period/monthly.

Example... (Either 10% of your pay or a flat $10 each week/month as savings)

Credit 411

Preparing for Credit

- Good credit extends into all areas of life and future
- Perils of poor credit (possible employment factors, housing, purchasing power)

Credit Facts:

- Today's actions can and will affect your "future"
- If credit is destroyed it will require time and financial improvements to repair

Credit Factors: (Evaluation criteria)

- Payment of bills (on time, late, never)
- Old/new credit (how long each credit line has been established or how recent)
- Amounts & Types of Debt

*****NEVER ALLOW ANYONE TO APPLY FOR CREDIT USING YOUR NAME OR SOCIAL SECURITY NUMBER*****

Budgeting 101

Spending Wisely (Accountability for your new salary)

- First determine "Needs" versus "Wants".

- Need is a necessity, required to survive. (Example…food, clothing, shelter)

- Want is not a necessity but a luxury—something you can live without.

"WISH LIST" (Determine how to finance the "wants")

- Additional "savings" specific for each new item "wanted/desired"

- Extra work, volunteer, barter, locate desired items via thrift or resell to receive at lower cost

- Work extra, save and "wait" for non-essential items

Practice creating a working budget

- Use realistic amounts for discretionary income (allowance, part time job, etc.)

- Use realistic amounts for expenses

Leadership Academy

Leadership: Pursuing a goal and inspiring participation while developing potential of everyone.

This information focuses on encouragement, feedback for self-improvement and opportunities to impart skills with others in workplace or other leadership venues via:

Leadership development/refinement techniques

Team building/Role exchange

Curriculum

Trust factor dialogues/scenarios

Exploration of Natural Strengths

LEADERSHIP TIPS

Processes/organizations can be improved via teamwork and inclusion

Take others along during individual leadership journey

LEADERS ARE MADE, NOT ALWAYS BORN

Stay calm/formulate plan

Inspire others to remain calm by example

FORGE WINNING ALLIANCES

"Acceptance and leadership" versus "Influence and leadership" (big difference)

CREATE DIPLOMATIC SOLUTIONS

Identify "win" solutions where everyone receives amicable outcome

Punctuality: Effective Time Management

- ❖ Once career is moving forward it is important to remain punctual in every aspect of life.

- ❖ Arrive and depart work or school based on scheduled time and scheduled hours

- ❖ Utilize only authorized lunch and rest/break periods as instructed

- ❖ Do not over extend yourself (taking on more events than you can easily manage).

- ❖ Commit to arrive earlier than start time of work/school/event (traffic, weather).

- ❖ If tardy, always extend apology immediately for delay.

- ❖ If absent, provide as much notice as possible for proper coverage.

- ❖ Seek feedback to rectify missed assignments/tasks immediately upon return.

- ❖ Consistent punctuality will demonstrate sincerity, reliability and professionalism.

KEYS TO EFFECTIVE TIME MANAGEMENT (work or school):

RECOGNIZE AND REDUCE/REMOVE DISTRACTIONS.

UTILIZE "WAIT TIME" (ex… if carpooling/public transportation use as study or re-organization time).

IMPROVE TIME MANAGEMENT:

CREATE A SCHEDULE

ASSESS AND PLAN YOUR WORK LOAD/TASKS/EVENTS FOR EACH WEEK

ADJUST YOUR SCHEDULE/TASKS DAILY (REFRESH/REMOVE ITEMS)

EVALUATE THE REALISTIC LEVEL OF TASK COMPLETION

TIPS:

If attending school, treat school like a job. Use school hours to maximize learning (time and tasks).

By using these hours as intended (class, study, completing homework) individuals will create more time in personal schedule after school hours for hobbies and earn better grades too.

TOOLS:

To-do lists, scheduling, delegating, perform difficult tasks first, organization, using time wisely

Technology (computer and cell phone features) calendars, tasks list, memo list, reminders/alarms

Workplace Ethics

After employment has been secured it will be important to understand the value of ethics. Ethics in the workplace are structured and unstructured standards of conduct used by employees to guide their actions. Examples include honesty, trust, fairness, etc. All employment levels are accountable.

The top rated employees are those who desire "more than a job".

Companies desire individuals who are not "salary seekers" but "satisfaction seekers".

These type employees want to "feel good" about their work and the organization.

Factors Affecting Ethics in the Workplace

CAUSES...

- Compromised Individual Judgment/Decisions
- Compromised company standards

EFFECT...

- Companies are concerned with an individual's poor judgment because:
- Compromised standards leads to lower profits
- Higher costs/prices
- Poor/Unsatisfactory work environment

UNETHICAL WORKPLACE PRACTICES

Theft, destruction of property, document destruction, privacy breach, disregard of safety guidelines, poor customer service, inappropriate behavior, gossip or harassment are but some of the misconduct that can be deemed as unethical practices and possible grounds for termination.

TIPS FOR ETHICAL LIVING

- Respect Others
- Truthfulness
- Fulfill commitments
- Leave a positive impact